Our Nature: External Landscapes

from the Eternal Nature series

by

e. smith sleigh

Artistrie and Associates

Poetry Collections:

THESE THINGS are a One Thing
OUR NATURE: External Landscapes
THIS NATURE: Internal Landscapes
MUSINGS FROM THE FAULT LINE AFTER DARK
AN AMERICAN STILL LIFE
VERITY IS RELATIVE: Emma's Memoir
Catch a Lover Falling

http://esmithsleigh.weebly.com/

2018
revised

for my daughter
Emily Catherine

who said,
"write, Mommy,
just write"

Poem Index is located at the end of this collection

this day

in the morning dusk
riding in
on dawn's breath

from the half sung past
into and forever
the future

today
pauses
on its journey

--e. smith sleigh

sunup

dawn breaks into the night
what will it bring
as the black
becomes gray
becomes yellow morning

--e. smith sleigh

signs

this spring
the lilac bush
in my backyard
did not bloom

in a few days

a golden leaf
appeared
on the front walk

--e. smith sleigh

collision

as I walked
in the morning
down the path
through the gate

I saw a butterfly
and a sparrow collide
neither was hurt

and they flew off
in different directions

--e. smith sleigh

migrate

the birds
have ceased
to serenade
the dawn
and me

they move on, you know
where life-giving Spring
is still there
to encourage
their song

why don't we?

--e. smith sleigh

sunbeam

beautiful butterflies
move
from flower to flower
from marigold to marigold
in a garden
of riotous color

I become Midas
as I touch
the golden rays
of morning
and the flowers
along the path

in this summer day
sunshine will linger
long after sunset
on the luculent petals
of these marigolds

--e. smith sleigh

battle of clouds and sun man

about summer's end

delicate beauty
after the clouds
begin

sun man
gorgeous
shine through
playin'
whose sky
red
and
warm
and true

--e. smith sleigh

rose

in mid-sleep
I awake in such a state
at three

I couldn't
understand it

but then
it dawned

Emily Dickinson's rose and bee
are haunting me

--e. smith sleigh

clime

shadow soldiers
come riding in
on
 horses made of wind

to fortresses of clouds
from
battles in the sun

--e. smith sleigh

late June evening

I watch
the mating dance
of the firefly

afterglow
in an evening
light and dark
are one

full moon
clean air
cool breeze
sensuous star gleams
bequeathed from a world's night
without end

--e. smith sleigh

precipitation deficit

we need rain

lightning streaking
through this endless night
outside my window
produces none

hot summer nights
no rain in sight

hot night jitters
moonlight glitters

another flash of heat
and a voice speaks
from long ago

--e. smith sleigh

heat lightning

an orange Halloween moon
stares into my window
challenging
this sweltering hot July night
to turn into October
and me
to-do-something-about-what

the moon light illuminates
my faltering steps
down the hall
and follows me
into the bathroom
where lightning assumes
the illumination
and turns the window
above me
blue

--e. smith sleigh

lacking a raindance

I am as dried
and cracked
and parched
as this year
of drought that spreads
across the land

has my mind created
these conditions
or am I swept along
with them

the land suffers
and I, in my egocentrism
can only read it
as a dream

dry, crackling summer
full of white hot heat
and head-throbbing
dulling
humidity
when will you end

--e. smith sleigh

orange moon

at the end of July
in an odd summer
without flowers blooming
and gardens growing

an orange moon
presides
over the hazy, dark night
that seems more like the end
of September
or October

because my chrysanthemums
that normally bloom in Fall
are trying to blossom now
and
there is that orange moon

I must ask
do these things indicate
the beginning of some sort of change
or
is something
preparing to strike

we armed the predator

--e. smith sleigh

deserts

I live
in
a desert of intelligence
and
like the lost
in a sand desert
I am
just as thirsty

parched lips
of despair
cannot be licked

oh, for the Sahara again

--e. smith sleigh

ode to the night

what is this bird
that chirps
in the trees
at 4:10
in the morning

dawn
is yet
to break

when does this
night bird sleep
and what is
the purpose
of its song

is it an ode
to the night
that lies so heavily
on us all
or
is it an appeal
to the dawn
that is yet to come

--e. smith sleigh

Olympus

arising without a sunrise
I awake to a thunderstorm
and lightning
streaking horizontally
across the sky

for a split second
through the light,
I saw mountains of air
and Zeus, the Greek
the Thunderer

the ancient Greeks
were as uneasy as I am
with thunderstorms

who else
but an ancient, angry deity
could hurl those
lightning bolts through the sky,
bellow in triumph
as the deed is accomplished
then cry in sorrow
at his anger

--e. smith sleigh

new day

dawn breaks into the night
what will it bring
as the black becomes gray
becomes yellow morning

--e. smith sleigh

Fall

reminding me that it's coming is imminent

Fall sends a dappled, slanted light
into my window

my memory is flooded with leaves falling
yellow and red colors floating through gray days
chilly rainy nights and glistening frosts

I steel myself and shiver
I must prepare for the cold,
for the disappearance of the green
for the crisp air,
and the shift into rapid movement

--e. smith sleigh

morning’s choice

gray day
I won't focus my eyes
but, do I want such confusing
endings
to such colorless
beginnings

then, too, tomorrow's morning
can always offer
sunshine

--e. smith sleigh

spectrum change

deep dark blue night
descended
quickly
it didn't have far
to go from gray evening
to black night
with one foot
in orange Fall
and the other in gray, silent winter

--e. smith sleigh

a twist of wind

the rumble of thunder
can be heard
out there on the horizon
that is changing
from gray to grayer

a wind is blowing
across the landscape
across time
in my window
across my table

a thieving cold tempest
will shake the trees
and deprive them
of their leaves
and me of the green
my senses depend upon

this gusty rumble brings
a winter wind to my gate
bare trees to my eyes
and a chill to this house
that penetrates
way down past the bone

--e. smith sleigh

lioness

restless
and
unable to sleep

caged
and
resenting it

I become
dangerous
in my thoughts

so I rise
from my bed
with
as much anger
as is
present
in that blazing sunrise

and

I'm just
as
unpredictable

--e. smith sleigh

appropriation

dawn approaches
with the roar
of a cricket-chorus

will this day of my existence
be offered to me
or do I have to take it

gray dawns
make me apprehensive

I see only shadows
and hear
the dull noise of
fossil-fuel-burning
vehicles started
and raced down my street

the drab morning
should provide
some hesitation
for those drivers
who don't embrace it,
or observe it

perhaps I won't either

--e. smith sleigh

not knowing

a blazing sunrise
arrives
outside my window

fiery
and threatening
it sprang-up
in that sky
without
a fortune teller
or
a soothsayer
to predict
the outcome

I can feel
the absence
at Delphi

--e. smith sleigh

desert night

smooth jazz on the radio in the desert
saguaro land
I race down Tangerine
drinking tequila in the dark

I'm going toward home, home is where
I wait for midnight and the turn of a hand
to lead me to write my thoughts

brittle cold desert night air
embraces my soul
holds me captive

wandering through my memory
like leafing through the pages of an old book
the words are there
but the pages are crumbling

mountains in the distance
look like banks of clouds
hovering
the living of life eludes me
oh, deliver me from stagnation
I want the joy again

lost in a mirage of the psyche
I convince myself
that that desert landscape is green

there was a time, there was a choice
I choose and I lost
ignorance is my excuse

I look into the dark
and can almost see
the shores of a lake
I smell the water

there is despair within me
and an unwillingness to continue
dry death surrounds me
the void is becoming a reality

empty desert sings
'drinker man's coming to
suck life from your soul'

night screams at the windows
sleep is overwhelming me
the cliff approaches

I struggle in my mind
to raze the questions and the currents
that could sweep me out this door

--e. smith sleigh

asphalt

blue
cars
slowly
driving
on the road
time rose
fast
on
a dark black sea
of
race and show
and
go away

--e. smith sleigh

morning dawns

a cold, steel grey
morning
dawns
on this tired
sleepy-ass
town

on this December
Wednesday

on this place
state of stupidity

on that old
house next door

on grass lawns
covered
with ice sticks
of frost

on my car that
is glazed grey

on my heart
that is cold

--e. smith sleigh

disconcerting weather

an annoying sunlight
appeared
this morning
in a early February day
that should be
cold and gray
in the depths of winter

instead the sunlight
brought 60 degree temperatures
in this mid-winter
offering only an awkwardness
and disruption

--e. smith sleigh

morning thoughts

morning comes again
with frost
and a strange sunlight
to push this part of the world
through time
and light

there's something
of an irksome presence
about this morning
it is steely gray
angular and bare

the cold is the hurting,
stinging kind
the air seems full of friction
and resistance

I want to go
back to the house
back to bed
back to summer
back in time

--e. smith sleigh

spring snow

ass-backward weather
is irritating as hell
two days remain
until April
snow covers
my lawn

--e. smith sleigh

theory or reality

as on Mars
the planetary DNA
the viral infection
known as humanity
is about to
lay waste to
another world, earth

where does it go
from here
which planet
does it
consume next

--e. smith sleigh

deity and a little cosmos

when I bent down
to retrieve my keys
a large crevice
in the pavement
appeared to me

it contained a universe
I had not considered before

unnoticed, it was thriving,
teaming with life
small plants and insects
uninvolved with the human

for a moment
I longed to make it
tamper-proof
but
I stood up
it was on its own

I walked away

--e. smith sleigh

hope’s illusion

hope
is out there
twinkling
on the desert horizon

it moves away
as I move
toward it
teasing me
it’s within my sight
but
not within my reach

curse
Pandora's box
and
all it contained

--e. smith sleigh

premonition

there were at least
a thousand instances in my life
when I knew what would
happen before it happened
have I created
my own illusion

--e. smith sleigh

night bird

at 3 am
this onyx night invites
a bird
to sing

--e. smith sleigh

sunset

I watched
the pink of sunset
rise in the sky
from an obscured horizon

as it rose farther
into the sky-dome
it met the blue
and white and yellow
of day

as the colors collided
night
descended

their blush
created the covering
on a well spent day

--e. smith sleigh

renewal

cool evening still and narcotic
invading my body
lulling me
caressing me with calm

I love the air that I breathe

feeling evening coming
sunshine paling
the shadows lengthening
sounds seem muffled
a hush falls
softening day into dusk

star shine
silently
moon light
brightly
foot step softly
from long ago

--e. smith sleigh

reply

I call to my lover
through a blue and silver dusk
and listen to his reply
as it comes running
through the gold of morning

--e. smith sleigh

light dances

there's light
dancing
on my fingertips

there's light
gleaming
through the morning

light
streaming
through the window
fluttering, flickering
into the room
to the mirror
reflecting you

there's light
dancing
on my fingertips
there's light
dancing
bouncing
off the wall
surrounding you

there’s light
leading you
through my gate

prancing
down the walk
leaping
up the street with you

on the balcony
the light dims
but is still
dancing

I raise my fingers to the sky

there's light
dancing
on my fingertips
light
prancing
swaying
gliding
bobbing
to my sigh

and our good bye

--e. smith sleigh

rain dance

come dance with me
along the plains
make it rain
why not

let's dance for
more
let's make it
happy and
make it love

come let's run
yes, let's laugh
ha
old world
feel us
dance across your chest

--e. smith sleigh

night quips

full moon
clear air
cool breeze
sensuous star twinkles

from a world's night
without end

I spent life
in a perfect day
doing nothing
enjoying
the sounds
of the earth

the golden sunshine
the laughter of my children
the sensuous heat
oh, summer linger here
and go with me
at my death

--e. smith sleigh

sine qua non

take my hand, joy
I want to laugh!

happy feelings

oh, beautiful day,
glorious jeweled night
and all the rest of the days
of my life
run together
like the gold of the sun
and the green of the earth
in the freshness of morning

joy, sweet, joy
take my hand
and we'll celebrate

here, let's drink
from the cup of life and love

I like happy endings

--e. smith sleigh

Poetry Index

Page | Title

24. lioness
25. appropriation
26. not knowing
27. desert night
28. desert night cont'd
29. asphalt
30. morning dawns
31. cold morning thoughts
32. spring snow
33. disconcerting weather
34. theory or reality
35. deity and a little cosmos
36. hope's illusion
37. premonition
38. night bird
39. sunset
40. renewal
41. reply
42. light dances
43. light dances cont'd
44. rain dance
45. night quips
46. *sine qua non*

e. smith sleigh writes poetry, fiction, and non-fiction.

She won recognition for her writing in the US and abroad. Sleigh was educated at the universities of Delaware and Michigan, taught at the college level, and has traveled extensively.

She now lives in Robert Penn Warren and Edgar Cayce country where she draws inspiration.

authorandpoet, twitter
http://esmithsleigh.weebly.com/

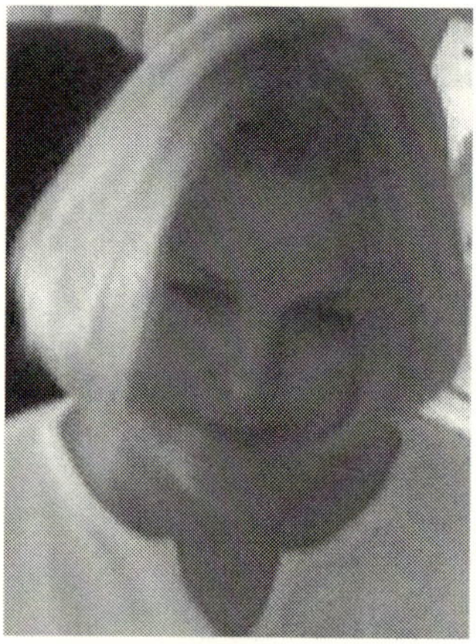

e. smith sleigh

Made in the USA
Columbia, SC
01 September 2020

17986662R00031